Praise for Joy ......

The world of education has shifted and educators are encountering challenges never seen before. In order to continue pressing forward, it is imperative that educators become intentional in finding the joy in their work. Dr. Joy uses the power of story to give educators tools and strategies to help them reconnect with their joy.

Sanée Bell, EdD, *Author of Be Excellent on Purpose: Intentional Strategies for Impactful Leadership*

With burnout rapidly permeating the education system, Dr. Joy's book is right on time. It offers educators at all levels examples of how to find and tap into joy. She shares her journey of creating her own "joystick" that helped her shift her perspectives about who and what controlled her joy. Her "joystick" helped her step fully into who she was becoming-her authentic self.

Rhonda M. Sutton, EdD, CPC, ACC, *Founder of Trust YOU Consulting*

You have the power to create your own joy, but it requires hard work and intention. I have been thinking about how to apply this to my life and work as I read each chapter. I appreciate Dr. Joy's vulnerability as she shares her experiences with bias, racism, and disappointment. She is a model for doing the work to create a joy-filled life. I also loved the voices of other educators sharing their own joy journeys. The reflective questions and exercises are useful for strengthening my own joy muscles. In short, this book is pure joy!

Julie Hasson, EdD, *Professor, Researcher, Founder of Chalk and Chances*

Joy Works is a tremendous book that every educator will benefit from reading. There are eight powerful lessons that share not only Dr. Joy's experiences and reflections, but also the voices of other educators who provide advice and inspiration that will positively impact you on your own journey to finding joy. Dr. Joy provides encouragement and inspiration that will empower educators to reflect on their practice and find joy in their work each day.

Rachelle Dené Poth, *Educator, Author, Consultant*

JOY WORKS

8 LESSONS FOR EDUCATORS

DR. JOY

EduMatch
PUBLISHING

DEDICATION

For all the educators who are fighting for their joy.

CONTENTS

Introduction   ix

1. Doing the Heavy Lifting   1
2. Engaging in Reflection   13
3. Identifying the Joy   23
4. Sustaining Joy through Challenges   37
5. Defining Self-Care   47
6. Creating Joyful Connections   63
7. Serving with Gratitude   71
8. Choosing Joy   81

Conclusion   89
References   91
Acknowledgments   93
About the Author   95

INTRODUCTION

Once Upon a Joy

"We need joy as we need air. We need love as we need water. We need each other as the earth we share. "

Dr. Maya Angelou

When I was a young girl, my father nicknamed me Joy. I'm sure there were times during my teenage years that I didn't come close to living up to this name. To be honest, I didn't even like that he called me Joy. Like many jewels that our parents shared with us during our younger years, I didn't appreciate it. It wasn't until I was way into adulthood that I realized what an honor it was to be called someone's Joy and how it was the one virtue that had the greatest influence over my life.

You see, as a young Black girl, I understood very early on that my journey in school would be much different than many of my peers and friends, and this was difficult for me to accept. I think back to sharing with one of my teachers that I wanted to be a news anchor like Lisa Thomas-Laurie on Action News. She looked at me and said, "Well, you're going to have to stop talking like you're black." I was in third grade, and to this day, I can still remember the sense of shock and hurt that I felt. I carried that incident through my entire school experience, whether consciously or subconsciously. In one way, it contributed to some of my insecurities about speaking in front of people, but in another sense, it lit a fire inside of me. I needed to tap into the joy inside of me to navigate the challenges of school.

I decided after high school to attend a Historically Black College or University (HBCU). I am a proud Norfolk State University Alumni. Having the opportunity to be immersed in my culture and witness the pride that exists as well as the exceptional accomplishments of Black people was something that I did not have the opportunity to experience during my K-12 years. Not only did that journey provide me with the unique opportunity to travel overseas as a student teacher, it also served as a catalyst for me to further my education by earning a Master's and then Doctorate.

Throughout my career as an educator, I have served in many capacities and strived to do so with joy. Needless to say, with all of the challenges that exist in our education system, it takes work for us to sustain our joy as educators, and more often than not, we have to dig deep. We carry so much from our pasts, our own school experiences, and even our day-to-day lives. Without some type of intentional work, we cannot fulfill our roles or serve joyfully.

I began writing this book not because I had mastered the art of being the most joyful educator, not by far. While people will generally characterize me as friendly and joyful, I definitely struggled to sustain my joy in the different roles that I served...and still consider myself to be a work in progress. Whether it was teaching elementary school, coaching teachers, or serving as an administrator, there were many times when I felt deeply discouraged and questioned my pathway. I felt myself experiencing long periods of discontentment. It took me quite some time to truly understand and accept that joy does not mean the absence of challenges and that I had to put in the work, day in and day out, to find, experience, and cultivate joy as an educator. I had to put in the joy work.

It was my pursuit of consistent joy that led me to joy work. I began reflecting on my career and the lessons that I learned about what it takes to serve with joy. I started collecting stories in order to share how educators exemplify joy in their roles. It filled my spirit to hear educators connect joy to their roles because it is something that we don't do enough, at least beyond the surface level. Talking about the struggle of maintaining our joy is a different conversation that requires honesty, vulnerability, and the willingness to take an emotional roller-coaster ride through deep reflection. You'll get to hear brief stories throughout the book from educators who serve in all different capacities.

My hope is that these eight brief lessons within this book will guide you to deep reflection as you navigate your role as an educator and that you will be inspired to embrace your own personal joy work.

Love,

Dr. Joy

LESSON 1

Doing the Heavy Lifting

"Joy does not simply happen to us. We have to choose joy and keep choosing it every day."

Henri J.M. Nouwen

One morning I was taking my son to school, and as I was pulling out of my driveway, I noticed a waste truck was on my street picking up the trash cans from the curb. Since the driver was so close to my house, I decided to just wait to back out in order to avoid any type of mishap. Watching the sanitation truck that morning took me down memory lane. I shared with my son that growing up, his grandad would periodically take jobs as a sanitation worker in order to make extra money for our very large family, but I remember his job looking quite different from the sanitation worker I saw that day. I watched that morning as the worker controlled everything from the seat of his truck. It was explained to me later that the workers maneuver what resembles a "joystick." The joystick controls a claw-like contraption that picks up the heavy garbage cans and dumps the trash into a large container. When I was a child, I remember watching the sanitation workers running down the street, lifting multiple garbage bags from the curb, and slinging them in the back of a large container that crushed the garbage. Once the workers were done on a street, they would jump on the back of the truck and a driver took them to the next street. I always wondered how the workers chose who would drive and who would gather the trash and dump it in the can. From the outside looking in, from my perspective as a child, the workers who were running and gathering the trash appeared to have a more difficult job because they seemed to be doing the heavy lifting. I remember asking my father which position he liked the most, and he actually said he liked being on the ground running because it kept him awake and that the morning air always felt good on his face. I thought back to that conversation, and admittedly I would most likely choose the more modern-day "joystick" option. It just doesn't seem to require as much strenuous energy as the system is more automated and, quite frankly, looks a lot safer.

Ironically, that memory is what sparked this joy work project. Isn't it funny how something so simple as an image, quote, or interaction can activate deep reflection? I remember thinking to myself that I wished I had a built-in joystick of my own, that is, a contraption that could maneuver, control, or remove any of my less than favorable feelings or circumstances. You see, I had been struggling to maintain my joy in my role as an educator. In the simplest terms, I felt overworked and undervalued. My focus had slowly begun to shift more toward resenting certain structures, norms, and philosophies that were embedded within the system and my role. I was allowing specific circumstances to have total influence over my joy. It didn't initially occur to me that I was the person most responsible for my joy as an educator, regardless of the role in which I served.

Understanding that I had to do the heavy lifting when it came to sustaining my joy as an educator was a complete shift in thinking for me. I also realized that this was a shift in thinking for many of my personal friends and colleagues. Whenever I felt my joy waning in a role, my default response was to attribute it to someone or something. That response accompanied extended periods of discontent and feelings that I just needed to be somewhere else or do something different. How often have you said to yourself, *I just need to do something different?* You may have had the opportunity. I know I have had multiple. What I found is that with each experience, some of the same thoughts and feelings that seemed to impact my joy followed. It was like as much as I loved my actual work, I found my joy was easily impacted by circumstances and challenges in the workplace. Those challenges came in many different forms and to various degrees. I personally just wanted them to go away, get transferred to another office or school, resign, or anything else. But challenges will always exist in our lives and certainly in our roles as educators. Joy is not the absence of challenges. Where our joy work comes in is how we choose to respond to those challenges.

Joy work is exactly that...it's work. It takes effort, a great deal of practice, extreme vulnerability, and a willingness to learn and unlearn. Most importantly, it takes a shift in thinking that requires us to move from *emotional rigidity,* that is getting consumed by thoughts, feelings, and behaviors that don't serve us well to *emotional agility,* which allows us to face our difficult emotions with courage and intention (David, 2018). What are those feelings, behaviors, and thoughts that don't serve you well? I took a short inventory of what they are for me, and while there may be many more, these are the areas where I continually need to do the heavy lifting:

- Impatience
- Frustration
- Inadequacy
- Discontentment
- Resentment

I can tell you a story behind each of these areas and how they led to many seasons of unhappiness for me as an educator. What I can say is that I am grateful that I learned the power of taking responsibility for my joy and the need to work diligently in certain areas. Anything that

I have accomplished has been done with persistence and a great deal of intention. I'm thinking back to several years ago when I was working on my doctoral studies. At the time, my children were toddlers, and my husband traveled often. Yet still, I wrote and read on a daily basis, participated in numerous study groups, and maintained accountability partners in order to achieve this professional ambition. I figured out that this is how I needed to go about my joy work—being able to have joy as an educator is not something that just happens under the right circumstances or conditions. We have to be ambitious about it even through the ups and downs.

BEGINNING WITH THE POSITIVE STATE OF MIND

Admittedly, I didn't always buy into the fact that joy was a choice in my role as an educator. Let's face it; we deal with daily obstacles that can fuel negative feelings and serve as breeding grounds for counter-productive behaviors. Personally, I harbored some serious anger in response to the ever-present racial structures that exist in our schools. Watching implicit bias and microaggressions through discipline and academic opportunities could some days put me in a depressive state. Raising children and realizing that they have to navigate some of the very same issues I did throughout my education can feel heartbreak-ing. Watching this issue on a larger scale compounded my negative feelings. Honestly, I was fueled by resentment. Conversations with my own children were what helped me shift the focus of my responses. While I wanted them to be aware of the realities of the society we live in, I did not want them to carry the weight of the frustrations that I was feeling. I wanted my children to feel hopeful and take sincere ownership in wanting to be a part of progress. I couldn't be a part of that realization or education if I was always in a state of anger about it.

I learned that even in the midst of my deep negative feelings about a situation, I could actually tap into positive emotions. This doesn't mean that I'm walking around smiling about the issue. It does mean, however, that I am able to self-regulate my response by shifting my attention. For me, it meant honing in on skills to have courageous and productive conversations, addressing issues, and serving as an advocate for myself and others. It also meant taking the time to reflect on progress and small victories as they occurred. I became grateful to have held certain roles and been involved in various platforms and opportunities to impact the thought process of others and even intercept certain unfair actions against students. Being able to participate in professional learning communities and book studies has also been a way for me to tap into critical and productive conversations about the topic. Anger was making me emotional and ineffective. Joy work allowed me to be on the side of progress.

I also have to remind you that progress is not hurried and includes what seems like many minor and major defeats. Being able to sit at a table of educators and articulate my thoughts about racially-charged discipline practices without crying from anger and frustration was definitely one of my first small BIG victories. I am a super emotional being. My joy work opened a positive space for me to strengthen my voice and shift from resentment to resilience.

Learning to refocus some of my attention certainly does not mean that the negative feelings don't exist or that they don't ever emerge with intensity. Our lives are filled with ups and downs and emotional disappointments and hurts. To even say that having a positive state of mind erases negative feelings would be impractical. However, Barbara Fredrickson (2004), through her broaden-and-build theory, explains how positive emotions can widen our perspective about the world in which we live. As we learn the skills to self-regulate positive emotions, we build resilience and resources over time that can help cultivate our overall well-being and satisfaction. We can minimize those downward spirals that are the result of perpetuating negative feelings such as blame, frustration, disappointment, guilt, and annoyance and experience more upward spirals that can help transform our lives for the better.

WORKING WITH INTENTION

What are those feelings, behaviors, and thoughts that serve you well? I took a short inventory of what they are for me, and while there may be many more, these are the areas where I continually need to gravitate toward:

- Patience
- Empathy
- Confidence
- Contentment
- Forgiveness

As I work intentionally in each of these areas, I notice an increase in my overall joy in the roles that I serve. I also understand that I have a ways to go and that joy work is life work. It is an ongoing process. I don't believe we ever reach this "so-called" epitome of joy because there will always be challenges and difficulties to navigate. I also believe without difficulties, hardships to overcome, and challenging life lessons in our work, we can never truly experience joy as educators. Working through the everyday expectations and challenges while keeping our joy requires building our capacity in specific skills, and it must be done purposefully. I liken it to when I was teaching first graders how to write. Some students would enter in September, unaware of how to properly grasp a pencil. Many did not have an understanding of 1:1 correspondence. I remember teaching them a strategy in which I would tell them to "clap for a word, open for a space." They would gradually learn the concept of 1:1 correspondence through this structure. I'd watch as they would sit at their desks, clap, write a word down, then open their hands to remember they needed to put a space before the next word. They would work so hard mouthing or singing the strategy. In the beginning, they struggled to think about what to do with their pencil as they opened for a space. Some would lay the pencil on the desk, others under their arm, and well, some in their mouth. It wasn't too long before they stopped needing the structure. See, the structure gave them an awareness of what they needed to successfully write and complete sentences on their own and eventually write several to create a story. This is much like joy work. As we work toward making changes and new shifts in our thinking and actions, it can feel awkward in the beginning. We will rely on certain strategies and overthink everything we do, but eventually, the actions and responses become a natural part of who we are.

We can't solely depend on and wait for ideas, events, or structures from our organizations. These efforts do not replace the heavy lifting we have to do as individuals to sustain our joy in the roles we serve. There are no amount of potlucks, awards, professional learning, or changes in leadership that our school districts can provide to help us find, experience, cultivate, and sustain joy in the roles that we serve. While the efforts and work to support joyful cultures are indeed integral to the overall well-being of an organization, structural shifts alone can't accomplish the task. We have to embrace and exemplify the work, and it starts from within. We have to do the heavy lifting. Let's get to work.

SELF-REFLECTION QUESTIONS

- When you consider cultivating joy in your current role, what is one area in which you need to do some heavy lifting?
- What is one virtue you would like to gravitate more towards in your response to daily challenges? How do you believe this will support joy in your role?

EXAMPLES OF VIRTUES

confidence	generosity	responsibility
courage	humility	committment
loyalty	flexibility	gratitude
forgiveness	creativity	patience
tolerance	kindness	discipline

Joy Work: Valuing your Role and Others

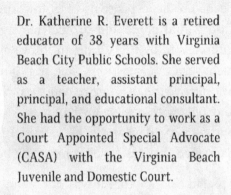

Dr. Katherine R. Everett is a retired educator of 38 years with Virginia Beach City Public Schools. She served as a teacher, assistant principal, principal, and educational consultant. She had the opportunity to work as a Court Appointed Special Advocate (CASA) with the Virginia Beach Juvenile and Domestic Court.

She is a member of the Alpha Kappa Alpha Sorority, Incorporated, and the Chesapeake/Virginia Beach Chapter of The Links, Incorporated. She is known for being a trailblazer of successful innovative programs.

I remember walking into my office with one box in my hand on the first day of my principalship, thinking, *wow, this is going to be an awesome experience.* I sat at my desk and thought about my dad. You see, my dad had been a principal for thirty years, and at that time, he was an assistant superintendent. I reflected on when I was a little girl and how I would spend summers with my dad at his various schools, helping him prepare for the school year. He loved the students, parents, and staff members. I dreamed about one day wanting to become a principal just like my dad. It was amazing to observe the interconnection that he had with the entire community.

As an educational leader of thirty-eight years (twenty-eight years as a building administrator), I am convinced to this day that it was important for me to think like a human—in other words, being a human first was key. I knew that I was not a perfect human, but I also knew that I needed to be a spiritual vessel for others. Every day I prayed first that God would guide and protect me throughout the day. I recall being interviewed by the Virginian Pilot newspaper, and the reporter asked me a series of questions. The first question she asked me was, *how do you start your day before coming to work?* I stated to her that I pray first and talk with my dad second. It was an incredible feeling to go to work every day and feel a level of peace. I knew that whatever happened that day I would make the best decisions for people.

My dad told me that it was not about me but about doing my best for others. So, I felt prepared. I already knew that I loved being around people and listening to their thoughts, some positive and some negative. But every conversation was a learning experience for me, and that gave me joy. Regardless of the circumstance, my goal was to support others. The power of listening attentively helped me value key thoughts that were being communicated. At the end of the day, every student, parent, and staff member would leave our conversation with a smile, knowing that I did my best to listen to them.

While serving as a building administrator, I also learned that showing appreciation to others was vital. Even when an irate parent visited my office, I expressed appreciation for the parent having the courage to share his or her thoughts. My joy came in many forms. I let students know that I appreciated them coming to school and demonstrating their best work. I shared with all staff members that regardless of their job description that they were the key component to the operation of the school building, and without their love for what they do every day, joy would not exist. Establishing community partnerships was exciting to me. I recall on the second day of my principalship visiting with the civic league president. She invited me into her beautiful home and served me dinner. She shared her wisdom, the history of the community, and invited me to the civic league meetings. I left her home with a level of appreciation and warmth knowing that I could contact her.

You see, joy comes in many ways. The ability to know how powerful prayer is or being able to communicate positive, inspirational thoughts kept me grounded. It is important to not depend on someone else to bring you joy but to realize that you have been put on this earth to share your joy with others. I am grateful to experience serving as an administrator for many years regardless of the challenges that come with the job. Every storm is a learning experience, and it is vital to take a few minutes to reflect on the storm and move on. My advice is if you have prayed about the job and God blesses you to acquire the job, then he expects you to fulfill the duties and responsibilities of the job. God got you!

LESSON 2

Engaging in Reflection

"Don't be so preoccupied with what is happening around you. Pay more attention to what is going on within you."

Mary Frances-Winters

When we begin to lose our joy in our work, we tend to default to one of four things: we react to it, roll with it, readjust some, or we run away from it, all while missing the key element of **reflection.** I can speak from experience when I say that taking time for genuine self-reflection can get lost in our daily hustle and grind as educators, although there may be structures set up for us to engage in reflection. Take, for example, our systems of evaluation where we have an opportunity to reflect on our instructional practices, students' performance, goals, etc. I've always found it difficult to authentically engage in this type of structure because I tend to focus on how I frame the language and how it all needs to align with the goals of the school and or school district. There is also an assumption that we are reflective practitioners, but the level at which we critically pay attention in order to learn from our actions can drop during high-pressure times. I've also found that there is a tendency to focus on the actions of our learners. Ironically, we yearn for our students, regardless of their age, to take this process of reflection seriously (ergo, the ever-popular think sheet), but may find it hard to embrace the process with patience and persistence. It can be difficult to empower someone else through the process of reflection if we haven't implemented it ourselves. Intentionally carving out time, space, and energy to self-reflect is integral to joy work and is a process that involves gaining awareness of ourselves, taking intentional action, assessing the impact of our actions, and making necessary adjustments...and...repeat.

Although time is certainly one major factor in avoiding reflection, another key reason is that we are not always ready to face this level of personal accountability and responsibility. Through the process of reflection, we can gain insight into some of our personal challenges and weaknesses, and that is not always comfortable. Let me give you an illustration. Some time ago, I felt determined to make some serious lifestyle changes. As part of this, I joined a 30-minute boot camp workout class. I went to the first class, and it was so intense. Although I was in pain for the entire week, I kept going, and I could feel myself getting stronger with each class. I went five days a week consistently for some time and then, little by little, began to skip a class here and there. Those "here and there" misses turned into multiple days in a row. After weeks of not attending the class, I showed up one morning, determined to get back on track. When I entered the parking lot, another woman who had started around the same time as me was getting out of her car, and it was visibly clear that she had been consistent with her workout schedule. She looked amazing, and I just wanted to kick myself for not sticking with the program.

After seeing her, I was determined more than ever to go full force. A coach at the facility suggested that I get a body scan since it came with the membership. She briefly explained that the scan would provide me with all of my measurements and that it was a great way to see a starting point and then track progress. I immediately scheduled the scan. On the morning of the scan, the coach walked me into a room and told me that I needed to take off my shirt and shoes. I immediately felt vulnerable, but I went with it. She had me stand on a rotating turntable which spun around as a camera took images of me. Later that evening, I received an email from her with the images from the scan as well as an offer to review it with her. I was shocked and, if I had to be honest, devastated to see this 3D clay image of myself. Just looking at the surface, I was disappointed in the amount of weight I was carrying on me—weight that I often attributed to having children and a very busy lifestyle. Attached to the images were multiple pages of information. I began to read the actual contents of the scan, which revealed more details about my body measurements and, most importantly, my numerous health risks. I had to come to grips that what was in the scan was a reflection of my choices. Now, what was I going to do about it?

Reflection involves going deeper than the surface level and viewing ourselves from sort of a 3D perspective. Genuine reflection gives us an opportunity to peer into the why behind our actions as we are confronted with our true selves. How often do we discuss the connection between the joy we feel in our roles and the environment in which we serve? It's easy to say that our joy is the product of our environment as opposed to considering the fact that our environment is impacted by our joy or lack thereof. Reflection can help us realize our strengths and weaknesses. Through reflection, we can experience true breakthroughs.

If we want to be empowered through the process of reflection, we must be honest and avoid getting defensive, blaming others, or making excuses. Our default will always be to blame someone or something. It's not easy to admit to our shortcomings and weaknesses. It is even more difficult to own up to the fact that our actions, reactions, attitudes, and behaviors can impact others and an environment in a negative way. An article from *American Secondary Education* described the importance of leaders taking stock of their current status by identifying which of their attitudes, behaviors, and beliefs could impact their effectiveness. A few of the areas explored include: identifying unproductive behaviors, attitudes toward change, beliefs about self-efficacy, strengths, and weaknesses (Zimmerman, 2011). Can you see how reflecting on some of these areas can impact your overall joy in your role?

Naturally, as educators, we spend a significant amount of time trying to figure out the thoughts, motivations, feelings, and behaviors of others—our students, to be exact. We work to elicit and gather truth and valid information in order to support any challenges we see in our students, whether it be academic or non-academic. We seek to know the why. We delve into their family history, gather narratives from previous teachers, and even consult with other specialists. We work diligently to shift the mindsets, feelings, and behaviors of our students. How diligently are we, however, with shifting our own?

Engaging in self-reflection is not easy because we have so many distractions. We move so much that we simply forget to take time to stop and think about ourselves, our actions, thoughts, and behaviors. It is certainly a challenge to incorporate it on a regular basis. I cannot begin to tell you how many fancy notebooks I have purchased with the intention of journaling at the end of each day. I honestly admit that I have several brand-new journals that have never been written in just lying around my house, in my car, purses, and everywhere else you can imagine. There is also this assumption that everything will naturally progress with time. We can get stuck in waiting for everything to change and evolve around us or for unfavorable feelings to just pass over time. Hell, I couldn't wait for all of my insecurities to vanish once I turned 40 (I am still waiting). For these reasons, reflection can often be put in the backseat when it really needs to be our front seat passenger, guiding us through the many roads we take through life and in our roles as educators.

SPENDING TIME IN REFLECTION

One of my favorite quotes about reflection is by Paul TP Wong and states, *"Time spent in reflection is never wasted—it is an intimate date with yourself."* The experience of reflection has personally allowed me to be less rigid in my thinking and more mindful of the thoughts that do not serve me well. In addition, it has helped me to gain a better understanding of my emotions, strengths, and weaknesses so that I can adapt to the ever-changing and often challenging circumstances that come with being an educator. Most importantly, it has supported me in tapping into more positive emotions. I can have the tendency to overthink things and have ruminating thoughts which makes me emotionally drained. However, when I engage in reflection, I feel enlightened. While that enlightenment may uncover something dark, I still feel hopeful and not stuck in a negative thought pattern. It's important to be able to identify thoughts and actions that are self-reflective and those that are intrusive.

RESERVING TIME FOR SELF-REFLECTION

There is a tendency to reserve self-reflection for milestones such as a new year. Thinking about who we are as a whole can be extremely overwhelming. It leads us to concoct goals that may not be within reach. Reflection is not about changing everything at one time. It's not a quick fix, short-term solution. Reflection needs to be ongoing and continuous. Finding a personal process is key. I could look on social media and watch people meditating in the midst of the beautiful ocean in an unusual yoga pose and glowing skin, but this is not the reality of reflection. It's not always a pretty neat and packaged process. There are times as educators when reflection can be downright scary and painful and may even result in those "ugly cry" moments. We may feel forced to reflect on our actions and behaviors and make changes based on circumstances, events, or interactions with others. When I speak about reflection as part of our joy work, I want to focus on how we can sustain it as part of a regular routine.

When I first began to really take reflection seriously, my reading life changed. Reading became a habit for me. I did not focus on finishing books or buying the newest books available. I found myself taking in information from a variety of literary sources such as poems, quotes, magazines, blogs, and of course, books. I always had a book somewhere near that focused on topics such as joy, happiness, and mindfulness. These sources provided me with "food for thought" as well as a way to enter into reflection. I was working hard to replace my negative feelings. Reading not only gives me an opportunity to reflect on my emotions, but it also provides me with positive strategies and thoughts to replace those negative intuitions. Reading helps me quiet my mind to the numerous distractions while making room for healthy and productive thoughts. Most days, I don't have an extended amount of time to read, but I learned that I could steal away five minutes here and five minutes there. These small increments add up over time to a profound impact. Working out is another time for reflection because it's a way for me to reset. During this time, I am void of other distractions, which opens the door for making meaning of my feelings, experiences, and decisions. I am committed to this time each day. It's important to be committed to our own process of reflection—that is what works for us as individuals.

What are some opportunities you have for incorporating reflection into your daily life? Here are a few tips to consider:

- **Choose a process that matches your needs and interests**. Many colleagues I have spoken with enjoy journaling while others find writing to be a daunting task in any form. Finding a personal process is the first key to sustaining reflection. Consider connecting it with an activity that you enjoy.
- **Tap into a thought partner.** Thought partners are those individuals who genuinely care about your personal and

professional growth. They care about your joy. They want to see you do well and will engage in honest reflection with you.

- **Identify guiding questions.** Self-reflection questions can start broad and become more specific throughout the process. Since we are focused on joy, a general question might be, How do I contribute to creating joyful relationships with my colleagues?
- **Schedule small increments of time.** We have to know ourselves when it comes to this area. Some people have to incorporate items into their daily calendar if they want to get it accomplished, while others do not. Consistency is key.

Reflection is by far the most important aspect of joy work. Whether we are looking back or looking forward, taking the time to observe and analyze ourselves can support improvements in various areas of our lives that will certainly result in greater joy. We will find ourselves being increasingly at ease when adapting to change. Our relationships can improve as we learn to communicate and comprehend better. We may even find greater clarity when making everyday or difficult decisions. My personal favorite is how it serves as a catalyst for creativity and being open to risk-taking and continuous growth and change.

SELF-REFLECTION QUESTIONS

- What role does reflection play in your world as an educator?
- In what ways can you make time for regular reflection?

SELF-REFLECTION EXERCISE

Spark Reflection

Use the topics below to spark reflection on how you are navigating your current role with joy. Make note of insights.

relationships	motivations	knowledge
emotions	values	qualities

Joy Work: The Heart of Learning

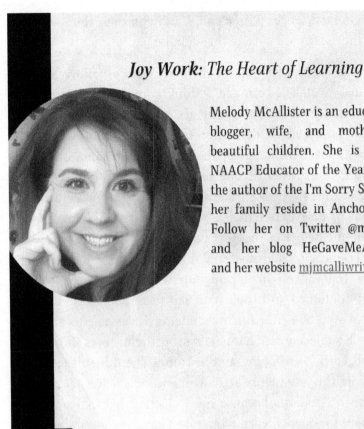

Melody McAllister is an educator, author, blogger, wife, and mother of five beautiful children. She is the Garland NAACP Educator of the Year 2017. She is the author of the I'm Sorry Story. She and her family reside in Anchorage, Alaska. Follow her on Twitter @mjmcalliwrites and her blog HeGaveMeAMelody.com and her website mjmcalliwrites.com.

Reflection has always been a part of who I am and how I operate in my personal and professional life. Internal conversations about my life experiences are happening every moment. As an educator, I learned that self-reflection doesn't come easily for everyone, so I also incorporate that into my lessons with my students, even with my first graders! When we reflect on something important, I've learned that it will stick in our brains for much longer, and we can build more connections. Implementing this as part of the learning experience for my students has helped me focus more on teaching practices and curriculum that truly matter for them. I ask myself if my students will think back and remember their experiences with a smile, and will their time with me help them as they learn to navigate through life?

Reflection also gives us a way out of the black hole of failure. Instead of focusing on a mistake I've made, I think about all the things I've learned from any one experience, and if something can be gleaned, then it wasn't a failure at all. Reflection helps me focus on what truly matters in my life. It helps me prioritize, so the important "stuff" gets taken care of first. For instance, one year, my students tested horribly on their state exams. I felt like I had failed them and my principal. I allowed myself to grieve, but then I realized that wallowing in that would not help me be better the next year. What could I do and learn from my experiences to help my students that were about to come into my class that next fall? I came up with a game plan about becoming self-contained and took it to my team and boss. They all agreed that it would be better for my students. I was able to go more deeply into each subject area. That next spring, their scores showed off all of our hard work of teaching and learning. The difficult lessons I had learned from the year before actually made me a better teacher for my next group of students because my reflection led me to ideas I could implement for deeper learning to take place.

Reflection can help you find new ways of learning and give you the confidence to take necessary risks that grow you and your students in the process. Reflection can help you stay true to your purpose, and through the pitfalls and victories, there you will find the heart of learning!

LESSON 3

Identifying the Joy

"Only when we pay attention to the small moments, do we make the connections that lead to a change in perspective."

Andrea Goeglein

There are many reasons to enjoy being an educator. It may not always be easy to articulate how we feel about our role or being an educator in general. It's complicated, right? I mean, we know the things we like, and we know the things we don't particularly care for, but some days we don't like the things we like, or we find a spark of joy in something that we don't normally find pleasurable (whew, that was a mouth full). For example, as an administrator dealing with grounds and maintenance was my least favorite part of the job. However, there were times when I could recognize how problem-solving and brainstorming about certain logistics made a huge impact. While organizing duty stations and setting up arrival and dismissal procedures were not the type of assignments that led me to become an administrator, I could see the value in solid structures and both routine and preventative maintenance. I also found it enjoyable to watch something go from utter chaos to smooth sailing. The thing is, we can have the tendency to acknowledge the chaos and challenges with far more intensity than we do the enjoyable moments. In fact, sometimes, we totally miss out on identifying or connecting the joy.

One reason we can miss the joy is that we expect it to show up in an elaborate type of manner. I personally spent many years pursuing joy through promotions, advanced degrees, and professional opportunities. I didn't always take enough time to embrace each opportunity for what it had to offer me at that moment, or how it was indeed impacting my life and the lives of those I served. My line of thinking was that if I worked hard and continuously strived to move forward and up, I would eventually reach the peak of joy in my profession, where I would chill and maintain. This perspective made it difficult for me to be truly satisfied for long in anything that I accomplished because I was always looking for the next big rush of joy. It's not a good feeling to realize that in hindsight, you didn't fully embrace a situation or role or capitalize on the potential joy that is in all of our environments each day. When we truly tap into the power of reflection, we often realize that the bad wasn't so bad after all.

How do you take the time to acknowledge the joy in your present role? It can be quite powerful to share these thoughts with others. Prior to writing this book, I began asking educators to share a snapshot of how they experience and exemplify joy in their roles. I post these reflections regularly on social media. Each reflection, while unique, shares one commonality—that is that joy is a choice during ever-present and ongoing challenges.

There is no denying the fact that it can be extremely overwhelming to meet the demands placed on us as educators. There is not one instructional setting or position that is immune to challenges, although our minds might tell us otherwise. It's easy to fall into that "grass is greener" trap. We peek at our peers' class lists and determine that they will have more success because they have fewer behavioral or academic issues to deal with. We assume that based on the location of a school, teachers and administrators have fewer or more challenges with parents and students. Most often, we compare what we perceive are the benefits and downfalls of certain roles. A shift in thinking needs to occur where the idea that joy is based on the circumstances surrounding a role changes to the idea that joy can be found in every role.

Consider Robyn Harris, who serves as a principal of a separate day school in Alaska for students who exhibit profound behaviors. Her school serves students who are not able to attend their neighborhood school because of behavior. She refers to her school as a "guest school" because she wants the students to attain the skills in order to return to their home school. When I asked her to share her joy work, she explained how she found joy in her students' ability to use strategies and techniques to cope with and navigate challenges. It can be difficult to identify joy in our roles when we don't see the value in what we do. In the book, *Resisting Happiness,* author Matthew Kelly shares, *Resistance will tell you that the problems are too many and that you'll never make a difference. Ignore it. Resistance is a liar* (Kelly, 2016, p. 25). This resistance identified in the book includes those attitudes that are self-loathing. We can't always wait for someone to point out what's good. We have to intentionally identify the joy. How do you do that?

IT'S ALL ABOUT PERSPECTIVE

Perspective has everything to do with the joy we experience. We can delay our joy by waiting for the perfect situation to come along. We have to envision the joy we want to feel and lean into it. If we can't find anything to feel joyful about in our current role, we will most likely not be able to sustain joy in any future role because our perspective and attitude will not allow us to. I say this because we can develop a habit of being dissatisfied, and unless we work intentionally toward adjusting our attitudes, that habit sticks around. There are specific things that can get in the way of us identifying joy in our role.

COMPARING OUR SITUATIONS TO OTHERS

There is a quote by Theodore Roosevelt that says, "Comparison is the thief of Joy." It is unrealistic to think that we can eliminate comparing ourselves altogether. In fact, in a certain sense, comparison can be a motivational tool for personal and professional growth. The issue is when we do it so frequently and with a skewed sense of reality—solely holding ourselves to what we perceive as someone else's greatness can be detrimental to our self-worth.

FOCUSING ON THE PROBLEMS

Often, solutions to our problems are simple and right in our face and, more often than not, wrapped in time and patience. We wrack our minds imagining various scenarios that can amplify a situation. Problem-focused thinking can drain our energy and motivation. Most importantly, it is unlikely that we can come up with solutions when we are so focused on problems.

SEEKING AFFIRMATION

I want to feel valued for my work and contributions, and I know you do as well. However, if we are in pursuit of affirmation, it can become increasingly difficult to find joy in our role when we are not receiving praise and adulation. The constant need to be noticed can also cause us to engage in negative attention-seeking behaviors.

ENGAGING IN NEGATIVE SELF-TALK

It's ironic how we can seek and even expect affirmation from others based on our abilities while at the same time determining in our own minds that we are not "good enough" through negative self-talk. When we engage in this type of damaging dialogue, we can evoke feelings such as stress, anxiety, anger, and even shame.

BEING FEARFUL OF FAILURE

Every single educational role comes with inherent risks. Change can be uncomfortable, but failing to take risks in our classrooms, schools, offices, and professional journeys can become an obstacle that stands between us and our joy work. Similar to a student being fearful of making mistakes in a classroom, fear of failure can impact what we are meant to learn and gain from an experience, including the joy.

On the other hand, there are attitudes and actions that can help open our eyes and our hearts to the joy that is around us.

WALK TOWARD THE JOY

It can seem impossible to tap into our own joy when we are feeling discouraged, unmotivated, and overwhelmed. This is when we need to ensure that we follow the positive energy and tap into the joy that is around us. It's somewhere and comes in many different forms. We can choose to migrate toward it or navigate away from it.

ACTIVELY SEEK MOTIVATION AND INSPIRATION

Staying engaged is key to being able to identify joy in our roles. Sometimes we simply stop trying too soon. We give up and resign to the fact that joy can't reside in our role or workplace. Seeking opportunities to stretch our thinking, ideals, and perceptions can be a great catalyst for joy as we unburden some of our hang-ups.

SHARE THE JOY THAT YOU EXPERIENCE

No joy is too small. Take time to share when you experience a joyful feeling in connection to work, and don't downplay it. Whether it is a small personal accomplishment or something greater, spread the word. You would be surprised at how you can encourage others to do the same. Know that the joy you share can transform an organization's culture.

FAVOR EMPATHY OVER EXPECTATIONS

Taking time to learn about our role on both an emotional and cognitive level will require us to drift away from our own highly-defined standards. Trust me; I know this is difficult. But also, trust me that more often than not, those firm expectations that we carry into our role can be the greatest stumbling blocks to our joy. Shifting our position on the continuum in order to place emphasis on empathy opens the door to joy.

REFLECT ON THE MEANING OF YOUR ROLE

Why are you an educator? Being able to whole-heartedly and authentically answer this question can be fuel for joy. Why we do what we do can be motivated by many factors. Truly reflecting on the meaning of our role changes our perspective as we recognize what a true privilege it is to be in a position to make such a tremendous positive impact on...the world.

SELF-REFLECTION EXERCISE 1

Over the next few days, complete the following prompts. Take time to capture the joy around you. Consider if you have missed opportunities to acknowledge the joy in your role.

I felt so satisfied when...

...really makes me smile

I have been inspired and motivated by...

I couldn't believe how good it felt to...

I am really looking forward to...

SELF-REFLECTION EXERCISE 2

Use the empathy map to gain insight and articulate how you experience joy in your role. Consider a moment or multiple moments. What are you saying, thinking, doing, and feeling?

Saying	Thinking	Doing	Feeling

Joy Work: It's Not Position...It's Positioning

Paulette C. France, Ed.D. is Coordinator of Professional Learning for Virginia Beach City Public Schools. As a former elementary teacher, assistant principal, principal, college facilitator, and current central office staff member, she prides herself on continuously learning and evolving in each new role. Paulette believes that it is important to be a light of learning and kindness for every person you encounter. She is not afraid of change and welcomes it at every turn.

When not engaging in the job she loves as coordinator, you can find her screaming at her TV during football season as she hypes her Dallas Cowboys or during basketball season as she supports her UNC Tar Heels while her husband and sons look on in amazement. Follow Dr. France on Twitter @DrPFrance.

Can you count how many positions you have held in your career? Seriously, how many times have you changed jobs since college? Were there times you felt that having those positions gave you a leg up on achieving in other areas of your life? Or, how many diplomas grace your walls? Let me count the schools...1, 2, 3,... I remember having a conversation with my late mother when I was consumed with pursuing the route to a principalship and completing my doctoral degree. She first asked me how many times I needed to graduate? I laughed and said as many times as I needed to keep my head and heart filled with knowledge so that I could help people. I remember her saying, "Hmmmm... Will that make you happy?"

For me, joy and happiness come from being able to help people. When I was younger, I kept thinking that I needed to be in a certain position to reach the people who needed help the most. Struggling students, teachers who needed to be uplifted, or non-certified staff who wanted to be validated all crossed my heart each day. Some days felt easier than others, and other days I felt stuck. Have you ever felt stuck? I mean, really stuck as if what you were doing was not reaching the people you most want to impact? I. Have. Been. There. I thought that when I became a teacher, it would certainly help build that path to helping all my students and families back home. I thought that when I became an assistant principal that I would build yet another path to supporting learning and teaching for the students and staff I encountered daily. Time passes, and then that itch to reach becomes stronger. I thought that when I became a principal, then surely the impact of making connections with family and communities would certainly do the trick. In many aspects having all those *positions* afforded me the opportunity to reach people I never would have. I ripped, and I ran between home, work, church, and school. I still, at times, felt that there was something missing. It took me some time to realize that when you don't find balance in your life, then you cannot build authentic and effective relationships with people. I worked myself metaphorically into the ground. I was given a major health scare that should have made me slow it down, but I did not. I continued to push even harder because I was in a position. I couldn't imagine not being in that position until I had to live it.

A few years ago, I transitioned from the principalship back to a central office position. Many people wondered how I was going to handle the shift. I remember reflecting on their questions and asking myself the same thing. When you are in a leadership role, there are such high expectations for your performance. You get pulled in a million different directions to the point where you might not know if you are going or coming on some days.

What I came to realize my first year out of the principalship was that it wasn't my position that made the difference. It was my *positioning*. You see, no matter what your title or position, you must be in the right place at the right time to move in the hearts of people. Not position... but positioning.... People from all walks of life are going to come to you with a concern, problem, idea, discussion, situation, drama, celebration, THE WORKS! The impact you will make on all of that will depend on you being in the right place at the right time. Your words, your deeds, your actions, and your spirit all make an impact. It is not your position, but it is positioning. Right place. Right time. I truly believe that God causes transitions in our lives that will make an impact on the lives of others. Positioning...where you or I have a need, and there is the person in the right place at the right time to make a difference. That brings me joy. The best part is that you don't have to have a title for that.

Joy Work: Joy Is Energy

Dr. David Geurin has served as principal and lead learner at Bolivar High School since 2008. David is author of Future Driven: Will Your Students Thrive in An Unpredictable World? He's passionate about leadership, school culture, and authentic, inquiry-based learning experiences. He's on a mission to help others find transformative purpose and build capacity for change and excellence.

David shares insights with educators through his keynotes, workshops, and presentations. He also shares his voice regularly via his blog, davidgeurin.com.

I cannot be my best as an educator if I'm not finding joy in the work I do. Joy is my energy to keep going, to keep striving, to press on when things are tough. No matter how difficult the circumstances, it seems like there are opportunities for joy in each day if you just look for them. This work is tough. It is emotionally grueling. We are working with children and adults who have a whole range of their own stuff, both good and bad, that they bring with them each day.

So this is valuable work, important work, and even life-changing work. What you do involves great responsibility and great significance, and therefore it also has great meaning. You are doing meaningful work. And that is a joyful thing. What you do matters. You're making a difference. So be joyful and be energized. You may not get the credit you deserve or the pay you deserve, but that's not why you chose this profession. You chose this profession to be a helper and to make things better for kids and for the future.

When I'm feeling down or hopeless or ineffective as an educator, all I have to do is look to our students and staff and be reminded of my why. They inspire me and make me want to be a better principal. And when I think of them, I'm reminded there are good things happening, there are little miracles all around us, and there are people here who will encourage me and who will encourage others.

I'm joyful when I see students at lunch reach out to sit with a student that is all alone. I'm joyful when I see students excited about what they're learning. I'm joyful when a teacher says, give me the students who don't like to learn because I think I can change that. I'm joyful when a student accomplishes something they worked hard for, especially when the odds were stacked against them. I'm joyful when we laugh together, cheer for each other, and listen to one another. And I'm joyful when we mourn loss and heartache together and share tears together. That may sound strange to think of joy in grief, but I've experienced it. I've held joy and heartache together many times.

So when you think about your job as an educator, keep this in mind. A big part of your job is to be joyful. I'm not talking about fake joy or pretend joy. I'm talking about making joy part of your practice. What makes you feel good? What makes you proud? What gives you energy? Those things are your joy. Think about those things every day. Do those things. Make space for those things. Increase your joy every chance you get. Share your joy with others. I believe every quality of a good educator multiplies with joy. And every school is a better place as the people there learn to be joyful together.

Last year a student started finding me almost every day to talk. And every day, this student would share with me every imaginable thing that was wrong in her world. *So and so gave me a dirty look. This person hates me. I'm stupid. No one likes me. I'm not good at anything. I'm worthless.* It was both exhausting and heartbreaking to hear. But every day, I would listen with empathy, and at the same time, I would make it my mission to make this student smile. I would try to give a compliment or some encouragement. I would look for chances to create some laughter between us. And guess what? This year everything changed. I noticed this student was totally different. She was telling me about the creative things she was doing. She was the one cracking jokes. I wasn't hearing the negative self-talk or stories of how everyone was against her.

Now I'm not going to take the credit for her change. She did that. But I'd like to think I had a small part in it. And I know other people were investing in her too. Joyful people were in her corner. And we're all working together to create a joyful environment. That's the type of environment where kids and adults can grow and reach for their dreams. Be joyful.

LESSON 4

Sustaining Joy through Challenges

"You will find joy in overcoming challenges."

Helen Keller

Think back to one of the greatest challenges you have faced as an educator. I immediately go to my first year as an assistant principal. I always felt like I was juggling multiple balls in the air and couldn't drop one. That year stretched me in many ways that I couldn't have imagined. Most of all, having to be vulnerable about my challenges...was one of my greatest challenges. There was a lot that I needed to learn, much that I didn't know, and I made an awful lot of mistakes. My principal would say, "It's your first year; you wouldn't have known." That's how I knew that I really screwed up. There was, of course, the everyday learning curve I experienced with being a new administrator. Then there were those major incidents or occurrences that could be downright frightening in the moment. The kind of thing that gives you that sick feeling in the pit of your stomach. I'm sure you have experienced various levels of challenges in your role.

The thing about challenges is that they don't just occur in one area of your life. They certainly don't wait in line one at a time until each challenge has its turn. That would be nice. Like most administrators, I also struggled with balancing my work, family, and personal well-being. That first year brought on a storm of unforeseen circumstances. My principal had to abruptly go on medical leave; my husband had to leave for work for weeks at a time; my son was struggling behaviorally in school, I was experiencing health issues, and on and on. I was truly swimming that year. I remember one day I ran into a colleague, and he told me how proud he was of me and that he was rooting for me. At that time, he had no idea of some of the struggles I was going through... and I never told him. I realized, however, that even though it was a difficult year, I was still striving to do the damn thing each day. That feeling of working through your challenges is empowering, and that's where the joy comes from. That is as long as you don't harm yourself in the process, but we'll get to self-care in an upcoming chapter.

Unexpected blessings that come from our challenges are often revealed in our quiet moments—another reason why reflection is key. I think back to how much I learned as a first-year administrator and how the role helped me grow emotionally as a human being. Have you ever made the statement, *Boy, if it weren't for that...I would never have been able to...?* Consider how your response to challenges may have helped you develop certain virtues, build a meaningful relationship, or deeply impact the life of a child. You have most likely built some thick, tough skin in certain areas, which is needed for life.

RESPONDING TO CHALLENGES

As we may be able to see the positive in hindsight, how can we maintain our joy during challenging times? I have to be honest and say that I struggle with this. I know this because when I am going through challenges, I have the tendency to retreat. I've worked on this diligently over the past few years, even speaking about it outwardly to family members who know my history of being "missing in action." I liken my feelings to a situation that happened at the gym one day.

I shared earlier how I attended this intense boot camp class. Well, one morning, I'm in the middle of doing these mountain climbers. I've got my rhythm, and the music was on point. The boot camp class was packed that day, and everybody was doing their thing while the coaches cheered us on. So I'm in the middle of my mountain climbers boppin my head to *Vivrant Thing* by Q-Tip when all of a sudden the music stops.

The coaches start scrambling around the room to try to get the music fixed while telling us to keep going. I remember one coach distinctly belted out, *"This is the time when you have to listen to your music inside!"* I'm not sure if anyone stopped altogether, but many of us slowed down or took a pause. We struggled to keep up the momentum without the music. This is how I feel when challenges arise, like I'm on a flow and my music just stops. At this point, I have many choices; I can keep moving, go on pause, stop and reset, or wait for someone else to hit play. How do you respond when you are overwhelmed by a challenge or challenges?

We always have tell-tale signs that we have hit a major rough patch. Those signs could be physical symptoms such as headaches and frequent illnesses. They can also impact our temperament and focus. Then there are those unhealthy coping mechanisms that we might resort to, such as overeating or drinking and finding alternative distractions to avoid working through the challenge. It is important that we recognize our patterns of behavior during challenging situations so that we can gain a better understanding of our experiences. Patterns are powerful and can lead to new discoveries, connections, and breakthroughs. You can see things that you've never seen before, almost like looking in the mirror for the first time.

While we may find it easy to notice patterns of behaviors in others during challenging situations, we have to work a little harder to reflect on our own. As educators, we are naturally proficient at reading others. We sure do get a lot of practice and learn through trial and error. We are professionally trained in finding patterns of behavior. And when we delve into the work of analyzing those patterns, we can find solutions that can help our students soar. Think about how much more effective we could be at responding to challenges if we did the work of analyzing our behavior patterns when addressing them. One thing it could do is help us come up with ideas or strategies that can support us in maintaining our joy through challenges. Here are three that are personal to me:

LIMITING NEGATIVE RESPONSES

I shared in the book, *Education Write Now: Solutions to Common Challenges in Your School or Classroom* (2020, p.9):

> Dwelling on difficulties can be a roadblock to improvement and give us an unbalanced perspective. While challenges bring a level of stress and certainly more responsibility and accountability, they build character and how we respond says a great deal. When we primarily focus on what we don't like or try to find ways to avoid discomfort, it becomes difficult to navigate a landscape where challenges and uncertainty are inevitable. Therefore, lessening our negative responses is key."

Negative responses can include such things as looking for blame, having distorting thoughts, being unaccepting of reality, engaging in overreacting types of behaviors, and lacking empathy and grace for both yourself and others.

PERSISTING ON WITH GUIDANCE, PATIENCE, AND HOPE

We would all love to glide through our challenges gracefully and unscarred. Unfortunately, challenges can wreak havoc on our personal and professional lives, our well-being, state of mind, and physical being as well. Seeking some kind of guidance can often lessen that impact. There are more folks in our lives or personal and professional circles that have experienced the same challenges and can provide insight. When we are adamant about hiding our struggles, we can miss out on rich support from people who wholeheartedly want to help. Along with that support comes the mindset that we have to be patient with the process and have some measure of hope that we will come out of our challenge stronger and better equipped in whichever area we are facing.

ENGAGING IN ROUTINES AND STRATEGIES TO HELP INCREASE JOY

Often, we stray towards habits and routines that can take away from our joy. We don't even realize that we are blocking our own contentment and happiness through such things as bad daily habits. At the moment, they may seem satisfying or just easier. For example, hitting the snooze button and getting an extra twenty minutes of sleep feels like a great idea until we find ourselves running late for work and stressed out about it. That decision and corresponding feeling can impact an entire day. As educators, we can never predict what we are going to walk into when we enter our building, whether that be a school building, college campus, or office. We are in the business of serving others. We cannot do this whole-heartedly without cultivating some very healthy habits and consistent routines. The implications of "put your oxygen mask on first before assisting others" are critical to the impact of our work. We will address more specific strategies in the upcoming lesson.

> One of the best ways I have found to increase my joy along the journey of education is to intentionally reflect daily on my own journey and that of my students. Where have we been together and where are we going next? I believe we often find what we are looking for in life. We can choose to find joy in the moments of challenge around us. Why not intentionally focus on the opportunity before us to grow personally as we impact the development of the students we have been blessed to serve?

Bradley Weaver, K-5 Music Educator, Atchison, Kansas

SELF-REFLECTION QUESTIONS

- What are some tell-tale signs that you've hit an emotional rough patch?
- It can be difficult not to let circumstances get you down. What are ways that you dig deep to find joy in the midst of your challenges?
- What are some daily practical routines, structures, or strategies that have helped increase your joy along the way?

Joy Work: *Digging Deep*

J. Kapuchuck has been an energetic and passionate educator for the past 22 years. He enjoys creating positive and memorable experiences for his community, staff, and most importantly his students. He has parachuted as an incentive for his students, rappelled off of the school building, been slimed, and even turned into an ice cream sundae.

He will do anything to bring joy to those he meets and wants all of his students and staff to be successful not only in school, but also in life.

Twitter: @PrincipalKap Instagram @PrincipalKapuchuck

In March of 2020, the education system in the United States was drastically changed at all levels. Students, educators, and families were in disbelief when they received the news that their schools would be closing. Most students and staff left school after receiving the news thinking this closure would be short-term and that things would be back to normal soon. Students and teachers left their personal belongings in their lockers and classrooms. For most school systems across the United States, the initial closure resulted in schools not reopening at all due to the Covid-19 virus.

As educators do so well, they quickly formulated plans to make sure their students' educational needs were still being met while learning from home. School districts provided differentiated items for students and their families so they could be successful. Packets of materials, school supplies, devices, internet or hotspot locations, and constant communication were provided in an effort to support students and families as they navigated remote learning. In a matter of days, teachers had to learn how to communicate with and educate their students remotely.

Even without training, educators found ways to bring joy to both themselves and their students. They caravanned through neighborhoods honking their horns while waving to their students, dropped off educational packages on students' doorsteps, and sent postcards, letters, and laminated Bitmojis to their students, in addition to connecting through social media outlets and learning management systems, all with the goal of supporting their students' emotional and academic needs. These forms of connection brought tears of joy to students and educators alike. Educators value the positive relationships they build with their students and their families, and these uncertain times have proven that more than ever before.

As educators re-entered their schools months later to clean out their classrooms and gather student belongings, time seemed to have frozen. Calendars reflected the very last day they spent with their students. Student work could be found on tables and hanging in the hallway, causing teachers to experience a whirlwind of emotions. Sadly, teachers gathered student items and placed them in bags so they could be picked up by families at a later date. This is not how any educator ever expected to end the school year. Usually, field days, field trips, graduations, and other celebratory activities signal the end of the school year. There were goodbye hugs, high-fives, and tears as students left on the final day of school. None of this could happen, meaning there was no closure for students and teachers for the 2019-2020 school year.

As educators, we are going to have to continue to dig down deep to find ways to bring joy and excitement to our buildings and our classrooms. Schools may look different in the future, but one thing is certain, the impact and importance of positive student-teacher relationships will remain the same. "No significant learning occurs without a significant relationship," says Dr. James P. Comer, professor of Child Psychiatry, Yale University. Educators play a large role in the trajectory of their students' social and academic success. Students are going to need constant reinforcement that they are safe and cared for in your classroom, now more than ever, before they can reach their personal and academic goals. So as routines and schedules look different in your classroom or building, ask yourself, "How will I respond to these changes and make sure my students experience joy when they enter the building and my classroom each day?"

LESSON 5

Defining Self-Care

"Nourishing yourself in a way that helps you to blossom is attainable and you're worth it."

Deborah Day

How would you define self-care?
I want you to take a minute to think about it.
Jot down your definition in the space below.

Self-Care
/self-ker/
noun

A search for the meaning of self-care yielded numerous definitions. Here are four:

1. Self-care is any activity that we do deliberately in order to take care of our mental, emotional, and physical health ("Taking Care of Yourself," 2021).

2. Self-care is a broad term that encompasses just about anything you do to be good to yourself. In a nutshell, it's about being as kind to yourself as you would be to others. It's partly about knowing when your resources are running low, and stepping back to replenish them rather than letting them all drain away (Hurst, 2019).

3. The act of caring for yourself when you are ill or to stop yourself from becoming ill (*SELF-CARE: meaning in the Cambridge English Dictionary*).

4. These are our daily activities in looking after ourselves. The process of looking after one's self. Avoiding all threats and issues that may make a person face irritable and uncomfortable circumstances (*Psychology Dictionary*, 2015).

Do any of these ideas align with your personal meaning? Take time to highlight those words and ideas that are similar to yours or you feel should be added to your definition.

Now think about self-care through the lens of your role as an educator. Is there anything in your definition that you would adjust? Take time to reflect on this.

NARROW OR WIDE VIEW

I spent a large portion of my educational career having a very narrow view of self-care. Admittedly more often than not, it became a priority anytime I began exhibiting physical symptoms from a lack of it. It wasn't until I couldn't seem to "come out of a funk" that I began to explore self-care more deeply. It became part of my conversation with friends, family, and colleagues. It became part of my reading and professional learning. I can't recall ever taking an actual course through college on educator self-care, not even a high-level overview. I also can't recall professional development being widely available in this area during a large portion of my career. There is certainly no shortage of sources available in this area now. School districts are placing a greater emphasis on self-care and incorporating professional learning to support it.

The more we learn about our self-care needs, the better we can be directed to helpful resources. To help broaden the conversation about the impact of self-care on our lives, let's consider the numerous categories associated with self-care such as **physical, mental, emotional, practical, professional, social,** and **spiritual**...just to name some of the most common. When we look at all of the areas in which self-care is required in our lives, we can better understand the impact of not tending to our self-care needs. The impact is not just on ourselves, but those we lead, serve, feed, and lay down with each evening are impacted as well. Lack of self-care in our lives can produce a ripple effect.

There are always signs that an area of our life needs care. Let's take, for example, practical self-care. At the core of practical self-care for me are routines. They are consistent structures that I have put in place in order to try to lessen the amount of confusion or chaos that occurs throughout the day. It's not the glamorous aspect of self-care that we sometimes imagine, but it's definitely a necessity that adds to my joy. Establishing routines such as the time we awake each morning may not always feel joyful, but the positive results will be evidenced in multiple areas of our lives. That's the joy work.

SELF-CARE 101
10 ways to take better care of you

1. Self- care means knowing who you are and your limits.

2. Self -care means getting the sleep you need and knowing how to rest.

3. Self -care means making sure that you're well fed.

4. Self- care means finding a way to decompress throughout your day, not just when you leave work.

5. Self -care means giving some thought to changing a difficult work situation.

6. Self- care means taking time to get to know you better.

7. Self -care means identifying what you enjoy doing and what's fun for you and make a serious effort to integrate it into your day or, at the very least, your week.

8. Self -care means knowing how to decompress after a day's work.

9. Self -care means feeding your spiritual self.

10. And finally, self- care means taking time to love yourself and appreciating that there's only one you and you're the expert on that.

(Baratta, 2018)

My mom and I have this ongoing conversation about the importance of routine to our overall daily joy. She is a caregiver to my dad, who had a massive stroke over a decade ago. She was always determined that together they would continue to have a good and happy quality of life despite what seemed like an impossible setback. The consistent routines she engages in not only knocks down doors that every expert said were impossible, but also gives her a way to maintain a level of balance and an abundant amount of hope for their future.

While our self-care may not necessarily be all about us, it is very personal, and how we define it is based on our circumstances and individual needs. Taking the time to define what those important categories are and coming up with those supportive strategies in each area have been useful to me.

Allow me to model using the category of **mental self-care.**

My definition: Avoiding or limiting distractions and thoughts that are not in harmony with the life that I want to live.

Here are my self-care strategies:

- Engaging in any activity that helps me to reset and adjust my mental focus such as walking on the beach, gardening, and working out.
- Getting ongoing professional help to talk through dilemmas.
- Surrounding myself with family and friends—they keep me sharp and encourage my focus.
- Taking a pause from social media.
- Podcasting as a way to share my journey and thoughts.
- Reading books, articles, blogs, etc., that discuss mental health.

I captured some of my self-care in action for you.

My strategies are conducive to my lifestyle, my interests, and my needs. I am always willing to branch out and try new things and adventures, but also understand that self-care doesn't look the same way for everyone. I love getting tips and ideas from others, but if I look too much at what others are doing, I can easily start to devalue my own process and progress. We have to be designers of our own self-care by examining the way we manage our lives through an intentional and iterative process in order to have quality and effective outcomes. Simply put, we have to keep trying.

BALANCE

Let's face it, as educators, we tend not to buy into the idea of balance. You know we take on the role of an educator everywhere we go. I think we honestly believe that this profession is exempt from balance. I have been with my husband since my first year of teaching. He will attest to the fact that throughout my entire career, through every position, I have always tried to convince him that as an educator, it is impossible for me to achieve any kind of work-life balance. I would always try to reason with him that in his position as a master electrician, he left his work on the job site each day, "turned it off," "powered down" (okay, enough with the electrician puns). In any case, you get the idea. It is normal for us to believe that our classrooms, schools, and offices can't function without us.

When I became an administrator, numerous veteran administrators would share with me the various health issues they were dealing with, surgeries that they had either delayed or returned to work too soon from, as well as the hundreds and hundreds of sick hours that they would lose or get paid way less for with retirement. I was strongly encouraged as an assistant principal to stand out by getting to work way before everyone else and being the last to leave. I remember thinking to myself, that's not going to work for my situation on a regular basis. I quickly learned that a big part of balance is not striving to meet everyone's expectations and actually breaking some "rules" both spoken and unspoken.

As a school site leader, I have been intentional in cultivating my joy so I can support others in creating and sustaining their own. Keeping a schedule and then rewarding myself with a nice walk with my dogs at the end of the day has helped me to create a work/home life balance. I have been intentional in sharing with my colleagues the steps I am taking to balance and fuel myself during the challenges that have arisen due to a national pandemic. Prior to the pandemic my mantra was, "My door is always open." During distance learning it shifted to, "My door is open from 8-3 Monday through Friday, unless it's an emergency and then I am always available." I shared that with the staff, and I modeled that behavior. Modeling balance, while encouraging and supporting my colleagues to find their balance, has been so rewarding.

Jillian Damon, Vice Principal, Chico, California

It takes a level of boldness to strive for balance. Just as it can be difficult to stand up for something we believe in, it can be challenging to protect our well-being, especially when there are so many needs. Think for a moment, however, of all of the challenges that result from not having balance.

More often than not, my balance is greatly impacted by a lack of practical self-care. Practical self-care for me means those routines and structures I strive to do consistently to limit the amount of stress I encounter. I struggle with both staying on task and being so hyper focused on one task that I lose track of everything else. My therapist provides me with ongoing strategies and holds me accountable to implementing them. My practical self-care includes starting each day by creating a list of what I can and can't control for that day. I call it my in/out list because I throw out what I can't control for that day. My strategy helps unpack my otherwise bogged-down mind. Entering my day haphazardly tends to result in me forgetting important things, wasting time and energy, and overall getting behind. The decisions I make daily impact my balance, and it is hard to experience joy when you are constantly in an overwhelmed state. So I ask, what are some of the important decisions you make each day in order to have a level of balance?

I offer you my one and only acronym in this entire book, and I hope you find it worthwhile. I surely have.

B - Be genuinely present in your role

A - Accept that joy is not the absence of challenges

L - List your priorities for each day

A - Adjust and readjust as many times as you need to without regret

N - Never apologize for placing a priority on your well-being

C - Create boundaries when it comes to your availability and accessibility

E - Engage in activities that elevate the joy in your life

The consequence of not having balance is simply burnout. If you have ever truly experienced burnout, then you are well aware of the fact that there is not a vacation, manicure, pedicure, or massage that can instantly remove its impact. Reclaiming your joy after experiencing burnout is a true journey. Burnout occurs because of both sustained emotional and physical exhaustion. Because we now function and work in such hyperconnected environments, it can seem difficult to recover in a space that is free from the eyes of judgment. Being aware of the warning signs and being proactive in creating the necessary shifts is key. Imagine the joy that comes from creating a level of balance. Maybe you can't see it. Perhaps you can't imagine achieving success within the realm of balance. As an educator, you can't achieve success without it.

SELF-REFLECTION QUESTIONS

- Consider your current state when it comes to self-care. Where are you? Choose one phrase and reflect.

My cup runneth over

My cup is full

My cup is ½ full

My cup is empty

Where the hell is my cup?

- In which area do you feel that you lack the most self-care?

SELF-REFLECTION EXERCISE

- Take time to articulate your definition of self-care. Begin to brainstorm strategies and structures that can support you across multiple areas.

Joy Work: Being in Tune with our Joy ──

Dr. Sheila Wilson is an educator with over 30 passion-filled years teaching elementary, secondary, and post-secondary education. She is an avid presenter and believer in lifelong learning. Dr. Wilson works to build the capacity of educators and parents in the institutions where she serves and through her consulting company AmplifyED.
Twitter @wilson1sheila
Email: drwilson@amplifyed.net

I'm a firm believer that joy begins on the inside of us. It comes from a place that we can't quite put a finger on, residing deeply and emanating from our core. Some of us are so much more in tune with this joy (I'd like to consider myself one of these people). But others often intentionally seek it out in order to fulfill that innate need we all have, whether we know it or not.

As an educator, I have found joy in working with people. I'm fortunate to have chosen a profession that I'm passionate about and one that allows me to serve others at the same time. Quite frankly, it's the best of both worlds! However, a national pandemic abruptly ripped away so many of my joyful moments. Amidst the fear, uncertainty and isolation... my ability to feel joy lay dormant.

My new reality consisted of working from home and taking 30 years of masterful face-to-face classroom instruction and swiftly shifting to emergency remote teaching via virtual lessons. Though very stressful, I eagerly embraced the process, learned new digital platforms, and connected with my families to provide instruction and meet their children's social and emotional needs, which were many! I learned as much as I could in a short period of time, used feedback from students and parents, and made the needed adjustments to improve my practice. Remote teaching and learning became a huge part of my life in both synchronous and asynchronous formats. While I felt really good about what I was able to accomplish, I was still missing that "joy."

I began to find joy in using my newly acquired remote skills to maintain connections with my social circle. Talking to friends helped me realize that we missed getting together and making memories. It started out first with fitness by getting on Zoom and doing coordinated workouts. After the sweat, we found ourselves staying on just to be connected and talk about life... the good, the bad, and the beautiful. We learned things about each other that we never knew and encouraged each other to pursue dreams, achieve those goals, and live our best lives. Our next foray was of the intellectual variety. I started a reading club so that we could enlighten our minds and expand our perspectives. These conversations took on a whole new life and inspired us to be more empathetic people.

I've been thinking lately about how joy looks so different to each of us. Just know that joy is what you make of it even in the least favorable circumstances. Even though we were further apart, my friends and I connected on a deeper level and gained a greater appreciation for who we are individually and the value we bring to our Sister Circle. The key is to recognize JOY in what you have.

Joy Work: Finding Joy in the Quality

Alexes M. Terry is an Educator and Instructional Success Consultant with TwistED Teaching Educational Consulting Company. She mentors, coaches, and consults educators who work with students in urban schools and communities. Through TwistED Teaching, her overall goal is to "twist the way we do teaching and learning in urban schools."

Alexes's book *REAL LOVE* uses her personal story and professional experiences to provide educators with engaging, relevant, and practical strategies on how to educate, connect with, and transform the lives of students, in urban schools, who see no way out of the conditions that surround them. www.twistedteaching.com

After nine years of teaching, I'd had enough! I was burnt out, tired of the classroom, tired of the students, and overall, tired of teaching. I was ready for something new. I felt it was my time to move on because I had lost my effectiveness. When I first began my teaching career, I did not see the profession as something long-term. It satisfied me at the moment, and it came easily. I did not enter the profession loving what I did. However, it was a career that I had grown to really love. When I invested time in designing lessons, building connections with students, and collaborating with my colleagues, teaching became fun. For a long time, I really enjoyed the work I was doing as an educator. However, here I was at the cusp of my tenth year and finishing up a second graduate degree in Education, and I had no more joy in me. I wanted out of the classroom and out of teaching, and I wanted it fast! So, I quit! I did what the old adage recommended. "If you love something, let it go. If it returns to you, it's yours." So, because I loved teaching and needed to see if it was me or if it was the profession, I let teaching go.

I thought after resigning, I could finally reclaim the joy teaching had stolen from me. Finally, I could spend time with my children, enjoy evenings with my husband, and weekends free of grading. Oh yeah, I looked forward to the weekends. Those weekends came, but the joy never returned. Instead, the joy I was seeking was replaced with sorrow and regret. The sorrow came once I realized that I had walked away from what really mattered. The regret came once I confessed that the true deterrent from teaching was not the quality of connections I was making with students and the impact I was having on their lives, and vice versa. Instead, what pushed me out the door was ALL. THE. EXTRA. STUFF. The lesson plans, papers to grades, meetings to attend. You guys know, all the extra stuff that really has nothing to do with what we are called to do.

After my second semester in teaching, I knew it was a profession that I was called and equipped by God to do. I did not take that calling lightly, which is why I was often conflicted. It was a calling that many times I did not like to do. But I knew I had to do it. Growing up and escaping a life of addiction, abuse, and trauma, I knew that God delivered me and gave me *my* testimony to deliver to someone else. I felt the hardships that I had suffered were not about me. My stories of hope and resiliency were designed for my students. When it came to education, teaching was just the means to accomplish a greater goal of helping students overcome odds and discover their purpose in life. I had lost sight focusing on the quantities. But I had to get back to my mission--my great command.

I returned to the classroom and reshifted my focus. This time, quality connections through teaching became the heart of *my* profession. I let what I loved go, and it returned back to me. It returned in laughs, hugs, smiles, support, and genuine connections with students. These life-changing connections reminded me that teaching is about the quality of what you do and give to others, not the quantity of things that often make us lose focus.

LESSON 6

Creating Joyful Connections

"The walls we build around us to keep the sadness out also keep out the joy."

Jim Rohn

y first year of teaching was full of surprises. I could have never imagined how many challenges were ahead of me... just trying to learn the ropes. I had an amazing mentor (Hey Sharyse!) who took me under her professional "wing" and, in the process, became a dear friend. I enjoyed the safety of that 1:1 connection and always found myself seeking that type of relationship in any role I served. I thought having one buddy to do work/life with was enough for me. When I decided I wanted to apply to become a school administrator, I spoke with a principal who encouraged me to move forward with it, affirmed that I was talented and knowledgeable, and also let me know that I was missing one key piece...a network. Although I had spent at this point a decade in the same school division, I only connected with a small handful of folks. I spent the majority of my time working in isolation. I hadn't taken the opportunity to tap into the most valuable resource in any school division...people.

TYPES OF ISOLATION

In the article, From Teacher Isolation to Teacher Collaboration, three types of isolation are described. Egg-crate isolation refers to physical separation. Psychological isolation focuses on how personal character- istics impact our social interactions. Lastly, adaptive isolation is described as the response to meeting the overwhelming demands of our roles (Ostovar-Nameghi & Sheikhahmadi, 2016). It's important to look at isolation from all three angles.

As educators, we are structurally isolated behind the walls of our classrooms and offices. Although we may be placed on teams, share similar roles, or work in close proximity, our day-to-day work mainly takes place in isolation. To add to this, there's a lack of trust and a "go for yours" mentality that permeates many organizations. Have you ever been told by someone that it's best to stay to yourself? We can avoid professional relationships based on a culture of distrust and our own fears and social apprehensions. In addition, the attention and effort it takes to create meaningful professional relationships can seem too much to deal with, especially when our plates are already full.

STEPPING OUT OF ISOLATION

While it's certainly important to be mindful of the company we keep and our time constraints, we want to be sure that we have not entered a state of professional isolation. It's a lonely place to be and so easy to get there. We often don't realize how lonely we are until we open ourselves to meaningful connections. Many of us have spent the majority of our professional careers in isolation. I, for one, wore the quote, "Don't let anyone steal your joy," as it was some protective armor shielding me from any negative experiences. I realized that putting up that protective armor may have shielded me from certain situations, but it also kept me from creating and maintaining joyful connections. Being "on guard" is exhausting. Stepping out of isolation begins with embracing the attitude that it's genuinely okay to need others.

EMBRACING DIFFERENCES

Once we have accepted the fact that we need others, we have to be willing to embrace differences. It's a major step to creating and building joyful connections. You know, we can be pretty tough on each other by focusing on what we perceive as another person's negative attributes or character traits. Struggling to see the value of diversity of thought is one major stumbling block to stepping out of isolation. Embracing differences can entail everyday differences in opinions as well as deep personal beliefs. It also involves understanding that we differ in the way we respond, engage, and communicate. We have differences in values and ideals, and we certainly come with varying experiences... and there is nothing wrong with this. We learn and grow from people who are not like us, not from staying around the comforts of what's familiar. So, who are the people in your professional network?

MAKING CONNECTIONS A PRIORITY

Over the years, I have enjoyed seeing the various celebrities on the Capital One commercials with the tagline...*What's in your wallet?* I think my favorite is Samuel L. Jackson. When it comes to making connections, we should be thinking along those lines, perhaps taking the time to reflect on similar type questions such as:

Who do I spend time with?

Who's in my group chat?

Who's on my calendar this week?

Who am I currently learning with?

Who do I engage with on social media?

Who do I call or text?

Who do I enjoy being around?

There is no shortage of ways to make connections. For some, connections are rooted within a work family. Others find meaningful connections based on sharing a similar role, while others seek out connections outside their current role through outlets such as organizations, social media, and conferences. And for some, there is a wide range of connections across the areas described. In any case, meaningful connections center around ongoing sharing and support. That is sharing such things as our resources, time, wisdom, and knowledge, and offering support through the highs and the lows. It involves showing up for others.

Taking the time to cultivate these professional connections can seem like something additional to do in your world that is already full of demands and responsibilities. We may crave connections but in a low-maintenance kind of way because we don't feel like we have much to give outside of our work and family obligations. Taking small steps outside of our comfort zone is crucial to building meaningful professional relationships. For me, this meant connecting with others who shared similar passions outside my normal network. I started following educators on social media who focused on topics that were of interest to me as well as participating in conferences and various professional chats. After a short while, I found myself being asked to facilitate various chats and presentations at conferences. I even had the amazing opportunity to collaborate on a book with nine other educators.

Through meaningful connections, not only was I learning and having fun, my confidence and voice as a professional began growing. See, others may readily see things in you that you cannot see in yourself. In that lies opportunities for professional growth in ways that you may have never imagined.

SELF-REFLECTION QUESTIONS

- What is one passion that you have that could connect you to other educators?
- What is one opportunity you could use to connect with a singular educator that has a similar passion?

Joy Work: The Connections We Make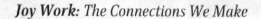

Rachelle is an educator, consultant, author, attorney, and keynote speaker. She is the author of five books and enjoys presenting on a variety of education topics such as edtech trends and emerging technologies. She is passionate about service to education and spends numerous hours volunteering. She welcomes educators to join her ThriveinEDU community.

Rachelle Dene Poth
Spanish and STEAM Teacher, EdTech Consultant, Author
www.Rdene915.com

For many years of my teaching career, my interactions with students were limited to the classroom and focused on the content I was teaching. My interactions with colleagues were limited to the quick conversations as we passed in the hall and nothing more. I was doing my "job" and making sure that I covered the material and focused more on the work I had to do, rather than the people. It took a long time for me to realize that I was keeping myself isolated and also keeping my students isolated from more meaningful learning together.

I took a chance and decided to have some students present at different technology conferences and student showcases. Why? Because I started to notice the amazing work they were doing, their excitement for learning, and I noticed a change in myself. I started to think less of what I did as "work" and instead, found myself spending time trying to do better, to find more opportunities for them, and to push myself to really work with them more closely to learn about their needs and interests. Learning was fun. Learning together was even better. How could I have missed out on this for so many years? Why didn't somebody tell me to focus less on content and more on connections?

Those experiences changed me. They led me to make connections not only with students, but also with other educators who helped me to create more learning opportunities for my students. Seeing my students share their work, receiving feedback from the educators and students they spoke with at the conferences, and noticing better peer collaborations in the classroom was an amazing experience. These students became a team; together, they set goals, supported one another, and became leaders in and out of the classroom. It took an initial step from me, but I realize that I only played a small part in their learning. I did just enough to get them started and then let them take the lead. This is what brings me joy and motivates me to keep pushing myself to do more every single day.

We have an amazing opportunity to start fresh each day. Reflect on the day before, and think about the interactions we have and the relationships that we are building. These connections are so important for us as educators and for our students, and they bring me tremendous joy every single day.

What I have learned from making these changes and that I try to live by each day is: *Every moment matters. Every interaction with our students matters. Find joy in those conversations, the laughter, the learning, and sometimes failing together.*

LESSON 7

Serving with Gratitude

"The root of joy is gratefulness. It is not joy that makes us grateful, it is gratitude that makes us joyful."

David Steindl-Rast

I f I had to choose the one virtue that has made the greatest impact on my joy as an educator and a person in general, it is gratitude...hands down, gratitude. Expressing daily gratitude will impact every aspect of your life, opening windows of opportunity that you never knew were possible. If you are someone who is feeling stuck in your current role, please listen when I say that gratitude is the entrance to freedom. For those of us who have experienced its freeing and transformational power, we understand that being grateful is easier said than done. It takes a conscious effort to not only feel gratitude, but act upon those feelings.

WHAT MAKES YOU FEEL GRATEFUL?

We all differ in how we feel gratitude. In the past, I mostly experienced gratitude as an instant and fleeting feeling. Something would spark this spontaneous emotion in me, and usually, it had to do with making it through a metaphorically speaking "storm" in life. We are more inclined to express gratitude when we are coming out on the other side. It's challenging to feel appreciation when we are in the midst of the storms and drenching wet. On the other hand, it can also be a challenge to feel appreciation when we're in that state of "winning" because we tend to focus on keeping those wins coming. I am striving in my joy work to view gratitude as part of my nature. This starts by recognizing what we are truly grateful for. So I ask, what makes you feel grateful?

THE GRATEFULNESS COLLAGE

One afternoon I started randomly taking pictures around my house...just kinda playing around with my phone's camera. I began reminiscing about what so many of the items had meant throughout my life. We had been in our home for nearly twenty years, so you can only imagine the memories and emotions that accompanied the snapshots. I can remember thinking about how much energy and time I had spent complaining about needing a bigger home and a separate office space once we had children and they took over all of the rooms. We had watched so many couples and families move out of the neighborhood over the years and would often wonder when our time would finally come. I had spent so many years being ungrateful for the beautiful home that had brought me numerous blessings. The tough times that my husband and I had experienced in our townhome truly helped build our strength, solidify our bond, and taught us the value of teamwork and consistent effort. I smile when I think about how many Thanksgiving dinners were hosted in that home and how I wrote my first book there while sharing an office with the dogs, the pantry, the half bathroom, and the entrance to the backyard. I did eventually have an awakening in my home, which led me to live in it as if I were already living in my dream home. And you know what...my dream home came soon after. Moving from our townhome was actually bittersweet, and that is a beautiful feeling to have.

I use this example to tell you that I've been in a role and work environment before where I was absolutely anxious to get out. I wanted more or what I thought was better based on my experience. The thought of showing up made me unhappy, and my performance and attitude really began to show how truly dissatisfied I was. There is no other way to describe it but to say that it is a sucky feeling. I'm here to tell you that if you carry those feelings and transition into a new professional role, you will feel emotionally tired and will not be able to enter that new role refreshed and renewed with excitement. Yes, you will, of course, feel excited about the new opportunity, but it will be difficult to embrace those positive feelings with so many unresolved negative and hurtful ones. If you don't change your mindset and just focus on your location, you will experience some of the same feelings of discontent wherever you go. As the saying goes, "Wherever you go, there you are." Gratitude can help with this.

BENEFITS OF GRATITUDE

When we acknowledge our gratitude and express it to others, we place emphasis on what is positive in our world. Gratitude is connected to greater happiness. In fact, Harvard Health published an article entitled, "Giving Thanks Can Make You Happier," which focused on how gratitude can help us feel more positive emotions, relish good experiences, and deal with adversity. The article shared a 10-week study that found that people who wrote down things that they were grateful for felt better about their lives. (Harvard Health Publishing, 2019). In regard to the science of gratitude, it has been shown to favorably change the body's biochemistry while decreasing anxiety, depression, blood pressure, and heart rate. Interestingly, research shows that true feelings of gratefulness can result in a more coherent mindstate (Shaughnessy & Shepherd, 2020). Gratitude truly impacts the mind, body, and soul.

CULTIVATING GRATITUDE

What are some ways that you can acknowledge and cultivate gratitude in your role as an educator? Have you taken notice of how others demonstrate gratitude? I personally believe in the good old saying, "Write it down and make it plain." I would encourage you to acknowledge what you are grateful for each day in some written form. Don't wait for someone else's disaster to acknowledge what you are grateful for. That's called being relieved...not grateful. Taking time to recognize something you are grateful for each day is where you begin to feel a transformation in the level of joy you experience. Also, I have realized that expressing gratitude and appreciation the moment we experience it is an authentic way of modeling it for others.

GRATITUDE CHECKS

Is gratitude something that you are struggling to feel at this time? If you are, trust me, I get it. It is so easy to be consumed with other types of emotions right now, such as fear, anger, frustration, sadness, and anxiety. While we may be experiencing this uncertainty in different ways, we are all facing challenges beyond our control. Before my feet even hit the floor in the morning, I need to do a gratitude check; that is, I have to immediately think of something that I am grateful for. Beginning each morning with a gratitude check helps me to enter my day with a healthier perspective. The only thing I need to do a gratitude check is, well...me. I can't wait to be inspired to find gratitude; I just have to be intentional. How can you intentionally incorporate gratitude checks into your day?

EXPRESSING GRATITUDE

I don't know about you, but I am deeply moved when someone shows gratitude and appreciation toward me. How many times have you literally felt disheartened by the idea that your students, parents, colleagues, or leadership did not appreciate your hard work or efforts? We thrive off of small acts that are meant to be displays of gratefulness towards us. They instantaneously have a positive impact on our joy and quite often soften our hearts, ease our minds, and help us refocus on our why. As you reflect on the idea of expressing gratitude, here are a few questions to consider: *How do I show that I am grateful? In what ways do I verbally communicate gratitude? How do I like for others to express their gratitude towards me?* Remember, gratitude is a skill that, once practiced, will over time boost every area of your life; it is the master key to unlocking joy in your role.

SELF-REFLECTION EXERCISE

Practice starting each day recording something you are grateful for. That's it. That's the exercise.

Joy Work: The Gratitude and Joy Connection

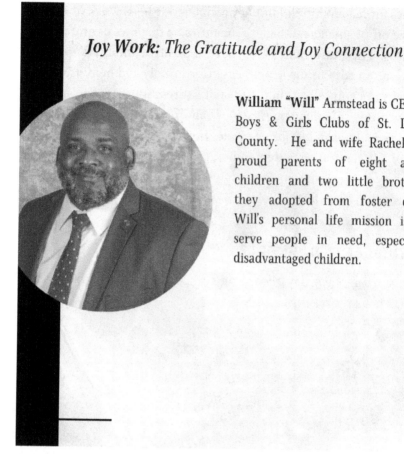

William "Will" Armstead is CEO of Boys & Girls Clubs of St. Lucie County. He and wife Rachel are proud parents of eight adult children and two little brothers they adopted from foster care. Will's personal life mission is to serve people in need, especially disadvantaged children.

Joy sits securely on my right shoulder. As CEO of Boys & Girls Clubs of St. Lucie County, I have the privilege and responsibility to positively impact 15,000 kids ages 6-18 every year. How could I not have joy in my work?

Joy infuses me with energy and blurs the line between work and nonwork. Joy wakes me up at 4:00 AM with great ideas. And then joy encourages me to blurt out these great ideas (many with seemingly impossible goals) to my 150+ staff. The joy on my shoulder insists I share my vision—to give every child a fair chance to be successful.

One of my greatest joys comes from challenging staff to grow, to do more, and be more. I enjoy working through the challenge puzzle, putting the pieces together—who can do this, what resources, training, materials, money do they need, and how can I connect them? As I receive feedback, I adjust the puzzle pieces and encourage staff to keep going. Finally, watching the team realize what they've accomplished and how they've grown professionally is a joyful moment.

How do I share joy with my staff? I know I can't make anyone feel joy in their work—that's up to them. However, I do believe sharing joy encourages others to find joy for themselves. I share joy by giving my staff the freedom, tools, and encouragement to reach their goals—and praise them publicly when they do. On occasion, their success is rewarded in different ways such as financial compensation or a special lunch. I find that sincere gratitude and recognition give joy to most people, including family, friends, and employees.

Joy Work: Being in Tune with our Joy

Demetrius Ball is a dynamic leader focused on serving his family and community. As a current middle school principal, he is committed to creating a climate and school culture that is welcoming and inclusive for all students and staff members and sees strong relationships as the key to helping students and staff thrive.

He is motivated by the idea that our destinies are linked, and he knows that his success depends on the success of everyone else. Becoming a connected educator through a variety of social media platforms transformed his knowledge base and has taken his leadership to a higher level. Because of his connections he has grown into a presenter, blogger, book author, and podcaster.

I don't know about you, but in every organization that I have been a part of in my working life, I have heard leaders say that they have an "open door" policy. I have had supervisors whose open door I would avoid at all costs and those that I would run to at any and all opportunities. I have always wanted to be the latter for those that I support. Not because I feel like I have all the answers, but quite the opposite. I read a lot of leadership books, and often the advice around giving advice states that asking great questions is the best way to help someone find the right answers. I think we all have the answers that we are looking for, and with a few appropriately placed questions, we can help others discover an appropriate solution. It brings me pure joy when I can help a colleague work through a challenge without doing much; all I have to do is provide the time and space.

I tell my staff that I have an "open door" policy, and I mean it. If I am in my office (I try my best to roam around campus to see all of the amazing teaching and learning going on, and you cannot do that sitting in your office), my door is open, and members of the team are free to walk in. I feel like because I am all over campus and I know a lot of what is going on, and I never enter a classroom or learning space with ill intentions, those "Gotcha" moments, that my team trusts me. Sometimes I see some things in classes that at first glance look off, but I always take a step back and remember that there is no perfect learning experience. Despite our best intentions and the perfect lessons that we design, things can go wrong. Because I visit classrooms often and ask questions in an attempt to learn more about my teachers and their styles, they are more willing to come to me when there is something weighing on their minds.

I have one clear example that really meant a lot to me and just confirmed the fact that I am doing the right thing. I had two team-mates in a really tense situation because they were not communicating clearly with one another. Each one came to me at separate times to share their side of the matter. I listened to both and asked questions to help them identify where they may have gone wrong. Both left our conversation heard and ready to engage the other about what was going on. They fixed their problem and are now closer than ever. The most amazing part about it is that neither one knew the other had come to talk with me! I like to say that listening is my superpower. It brings me so much joy to know that I am living out what I have been called to do, and coaching through active, intentional listening. My door is always open.

LESSON 8

Choosing Joy

"Joy is a decision, a really brave one, about how you are going to respond to life. "

Wes Stafford

We have the freedom to cultivate, experience, and exemplify joy in our roles as educators, even in times of uncertainty. Who would have thought that we would have ended the 2019-2020 school year quarantined due to a pandemic? Living directly across the street from an elementary school at the time, I had to get used to the sudden quiet mornings and afternoons. It felt empty without the sound of the students laughing and screaming on the playground or the busyness of arrival and dismissal. I missed my morning chats with my neighborhood crossing guard and even the cars that lined my street, sometimes blocking my front yard.

As schools began to gradually reopen in my area, there was such a cloud of uncertainty about safety. Even as I write this page, I am not sure how my own children will navigate school from here on out. Facing educators are the overwhelming issues of physical safety, equity, and deep-rooted concerns about the lack of value felt throughout the profession. Most importantly, there are multiple schools of thought, a clear division, on some of the most fundamental issues impacting our schools.

Throughout these last few years, I've questioned the relevance of my work. I remember so many times thinking to myself, "No one is trying to hear anything about joy right now." However, as I engage in my joy work, I am always somehow reminded of the importance of joy to any role in which we may serve and at any time. In fact, we are starving for it.

What will it mean for you to choose joy in your role? I'm talking about really choosing joy. This is not just about the smile we sometimes plaster on our face to make everyone feel comfortable. I completely understand that is part of what we do. You know our role as educators requires a great deal of emotional labor. That is, we deliberately suppress or express our emotions based on what is expected of us by the organizations in which we serve (Tosten & Toprak, 2017). Just consider this example. You are a classroom teacher in the middle of an amazing lesson with your students. They are fully engaged and truly demonstrate knowledge of the concepts being taught. Everyone is working well together, and you are ready to move on to your assessment when your door flies open, and your principal is standing there with a new student. How do you feel and what do you do? You certainly don't acknowledge how you've just lost your momentum. No, you put on that smile and welcome that new student like they are the best thing you've seen all day. During these times, we will have to engage in emotional labor as we work with our communities. However, we cannot lose sight of the importance of recognizing how we feel as well as advocating for our own well-being. Furthermore, it is essential that we act as diligent participants in keeping those actions and emotions that can hold us captive or send us in a negative tailspin at bay. They will not be productive during the most challenging of times. We will have to take agency over our joy.

AGENCY AND JOY WORK

There is not a step-by-step guide when it comes to joy work, but this idea of **agency** is the common denominator for everyone. Let's take a moment to examine this word agency as we often associate it with student learning. Sean Michael Morris provides such a sound description of agency when he says, "Agency does not give us power over another, but it gives us mastery over ourselves" (quoted in Richardson, 2019, p. 15). On the topic of developing learner agency, Bray and McClaskey (2017) share, "We have agency when we feel in control of things that happen around us, and we feel that we can influence events" (p.35). While everything around us may abruptly shift, we can maintain control over how we respond, and that certainly impacts our environments. The authors go on to describe seven elements of learner agency, including voice, choice, engagement, motivation, ownership, purpose, and self-efficacy. Interestingly, I have found that these elements align very well to joy work:

VOICE

Developing our external voice is one of the most courageous aspects of joy work. Employees often hesitate to speak up at work for fear of some kind of backlash. There may be factors in our work setting that can make us feel uncomfortable expressing our feelings and desires daily. When we engage our voice, we can impact organizational outcomes by improving student and staff performance and increasing innovation. Discovering the value of our voice as opposed to settling on "being heard" can provide us with great inspiration. Even more important is the development of a positive inner voice, which helps us discover and tap into joy in challenging situations.

CHOICE

We have the ability to direct our own professional pathway and are not merely participants in our roles but designers in the outcomes of these experiences. While there is a myriad of choices, and we can elicit the support of thought partners and mentors to help guide us and provide advice, we should eventually choose our pathway based on our passions, interests, and talents. Too often, we allow ourselves to become complicit, or we wait for opportunities based on how things "have always been done." We may not have control over everything, but we can always take charge of our professional growth. Never be afraid to change. Some of the most joyful experiences come from being bold and taking an unlikely route.

ENGAGEMENT

When we are engaged in the heavy lifting of our joy work, we become immersed in pursuing our passion and purpose as opposed to being compliant "doers." We are continuously discovering more about ourselves and how we navigate situations, and learn to employ tools and strategies to help us engage effectively. Through healthy and meaningful social interactions, we learn to value differences and appreciate the lessons learned, even the difficult ones. Never underestimate the amount of energy and courage it takes to be engaged.

MOTIVATION

Our emphasis is either on intrinsic or extrinsic motivation. When we rely heavily on extrinsic motivation, we tend to yearn for affirmation from colleagues and those who are in supervisory roles. We may have a difficult time finding joy in our role without it. There certainly isn't anything wrong with wanting to feel valued for our contributions, but investing in our role because it is personally rewarding is more sustainable. Understandably there are times we will certainly have a decrease in motivation, but we develop a stick-with-it attitude. We can gain a great deal of satisfaction from pursuing those things that have a personal meaning to us as well as a positive impact on humanity.

PURPOSE

Having a sense of purpose in our role is the ultimate level of fulfillment. That is, we understand the impact of our work and believe that we are making a meaningful difference. We have joy from understanding that our role is bigger than us, and we intentionally look for those moments to make positive connections, whether big or small. There is power that comes with purpose. When we don't have it, we become more vulnerable to negative emotions. Years ago, during a professional meeting, all of us participants were asked, "What do you want your legacy in this position to be?" That is a deep question. To help define your purpose, consider what you want to leave to the people that come after you.

SELF-EFFICACY

My joy work journey has involved a significant amount of unlearning. Many of my attitudes and actions were a result of a lack of confidence. I had to learn how to believe in myself. Self-efficacy serves as a springboard for joy work because it all begins with the belief that we have the ability to shift our responses to circumstances and not let circumstances shift our joy.

OWNERSHIP

Taking ownership over our joy simply means accepting personal responsibility. This quite often requires us to separate our feelings from facts because you know we tell ourselves all types of stories about "who dun it." Gaining an understanding of how our actions impact our joy can be accomplished through reflection, where we can authentically consider our **attitudes, assumptions, and actions**. You can't share ownership of your joy. You are the sole proprietor.

SELF-REFLECTION EXERCISE

Agency and Joy Work

Use the chart below to begin to brainstorm ways you can demonstrate agency over your joy work.

- Voice
- Choice
- Engagement
- Motivation
- Purpose
- Self-Efficacy
- Ownership

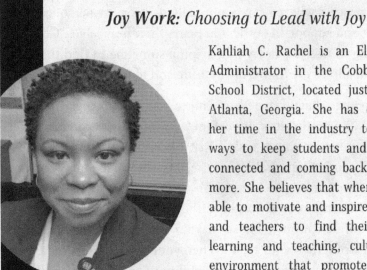

Joy Work: Choosing to Lead with Joy

Kahliah C. Rachel is an Elementary Administrator in the Cobb County School District, located just west of Atlanta, Georgia. She has dedicated her time in the industry to finding ways to keep students and teachers connected and coming back to learn more. She believes that when you are able to motivate and inspire students and teachers to find their joy in learning and teaching, cultivate an environment that promotes change and creativity.

She looks forward to catching you in the #LearningZone, a phrase she often uses to let staff and students know she looks forward to learning alongside them daily.

Within the course of a day, many things take place that can zap all the positive energy right out of you, from a phone call to an unexpected encounter, to a meeting that didn't quite turn out as planned. However, I want to offer to you that it is how you choose to respond in those moments that allows you to create the energy that is needed to push through. That energy that you create is the joy that has always been inside of you and the reason you show up every day to do the work for which you are passionate.

Why do I choose joy? People and their well-being are my currency. I have repeatedly noticed that the joy found in my day-to-day grind comes from how others see themselves and the impact that they have in the way they serve. When I am invited to support growth or change, it is in this process where I can continually develop my personal joy by influencing and supporting others in being their best selves. Coaching and uplifting in this journey while helping someone to find their best fit on a team allows me to live my best life and to increase my joy.

Over the years, I have learned to find joy in every experience. As a building administrator, it is important to look for the good in others and assume positive intent, a skill that I was taught and continue to uphold and value. When problems arise, it is our job to empower those in the situation and guide them with the necessary tools to drive a successful outcome. When you have the ability to lead fearlessly and pass that confidence on to those in your charge, you, in turn, grow leaders and strengthen your team. When your leadership is valued and seen as a support system, your team's ability to grow is endless. This is the outcome of creating the mindset that joy is a tool that will see you through any tough situation.

Finally, I suppose I've learned that it truly is the simple things that help create lasting memories, power your influence, and allow you to experience daily joy that will help guide your decisions. There is no magic behind it, no formula that I can jot down; it is just the pure practice of being intentional and the ability to see beyond your personal needs. Being able to give to others is where joy is found. The journey starts and ends with how we choose to live our lives every second of every day.

CONCLUSION

Joy, A Very Brave Choice

For those of us who say we believe in the power of joy, we are truly being challenged to walk that walk. It's not easy. During these trying times, the demands being placed on educators are continuously increasing while our faith in the systems we serve may be waning. There are such tremendous issues at hand, and oftentimes joy seems to be thrown around like a fleeting idea. It's unsuccessfully used as a cure and not as an effective prevention. Being an educator is a mentally, emotionally, and physically demanding job and attempting to navigate it without joy is detrimental to all three of those areas. My hope for you is that you will use the lessons learned throughout this book to place joy at the forefront of your role. Sustaining joy during these times is not just a choice; it's a very brave one indeed.

REFERENCES

Baratta, M. (2018). *Self- Care 101*. (2018).
Psychology Today. https://www.psychologyto-
day.com/us/blog/skinny-revisit-
ed/201805/self-care-101

Bray, B., & Mcclaskey, K. (2017). *How to personalize
learning: A guide for getting started and going
deeper*. Corwin, A Sage Publishing Company.

David, S. (2018). *Emotional agility*. Penguin USA.

Fredrickson, B.L. (2004). The broaden-and-build
theory of positive emotions. *Philosophical
Transactions: Biological Sciences*, 359(1449),
1367–1377.

Hurst, K (2019.) *What is self-care and why is caring
about yourself important?* https://www.thela-
wofattraction.com/self-care-tips/

Harvard Health. (2021, August 21). *Giving thanks
can make you happier*. https:www.health.har-
vard.edu/healthbeat/giving-thanks-can-make-
you-happier

Lucas, L. J. (2018). Modeling mindfulness by prac-
ticing presence. *Exchange (19460406), 240*,
85–88.

Ostovar-Nameghi, S. A., & Sheikhahmadi, M. (2016). From teacher isolation to teacher collaboration: Theoretical perspectives and empirical findings. *English Language Teaching,* 9(5), 197–205.

Richardson, W. (2019). Sparking student agency with technology: Why should kids have to wait until after school to do amazing things with technology? *Educational Leadership,* 76(5), 12–18.

Shaughnessy, M., & Shepherd, J. (2020). Gratitude. *Salem Press Encyclopedia of Health.*

Taking Care of Yourself. (2021, September 13). Retrieved from https://www.studenthealth.virginia.edu/taking-care-yourself

Tosten, R., & Toprak, M. (2017). Positive psychological capital and emotional labor: A study in educational organizations. *Cogent Education,* 4(1), 1301012.

Zimmerman, J. A. (2011). Principals preparing for change: The importance of reflection and professional learning. *American Secondary Education,* 39(2), 107–114.

ACKNOWLEDGEMENTS

I would like to thank Dr. Sarah Thomas for creating a platform that values and amplifies diverse voices in the field of education. I am grateful to the passionate educators who offered their reflections to this project and provided feedback through the process. To Eric, Erica and Christopher, I love you. I am honored to call you my family. What we have is so very special. God knew exactly what I needed. To my mom and dad, I could never thank you enough. The nickname "Joy" has always been a gift, even when I didn't know it. To my six siblings, Lisa, William, Cheryl, Kathy, Erick, and Vanessa, you mean the world to me. Thank you for always encouraging my dreams. To Zhane Owen, I love you my angel.

ABOUT THE AUTHOR

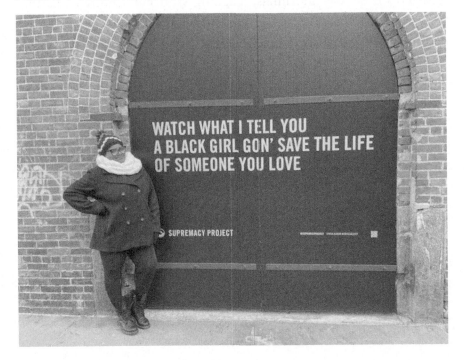

Dr. Joy is the Founder of Joy Work EDU, an Author, and Educational Leader. She is passionate about the presence of joy in schools. Her goal is to encourage educators to tap into the power of joy and believe in its positive impact on every aspect of education. She facilitates her work through the lens of joy, and brings her experience as a teacher, school administrator, and professional learning leader to help delve into topics such as coping skills. By incorporating elements of design thinking into her professional learning sessions, Dr. Joy offers her participants an authentic and personalized experience.

Dr. Joy earned a Master's of Arts in Teaching Degree and a Doctorate in Educational Administration and Supervision. She currently serves in a Teacher's College where she is able to bring her gift of joy to the work of supporting and mentoring aspiring special education teachers. When she is not working, she most enjoys having coffee with her husband on Sunday mornings, laughing with her children, chatting with her six siblings through group texts, and spending time with her dad and mom on any day of the week.

PUBLISHING

Made in the USA
Middletown, DE
18 March 2022